THE
GREAT BRITISH

THE GREAT BRITISH

Introduction by George Perry

New York Graphic Society
Boston

PHOTOGRAPHS BY
ARNOLD NEWMAN

Photographs copyright © 1979 by Arnold Newman

Text copyright © 1979 by The Sunday Times (London)

International Standard Book Number: 0–8212–0754–7
Library of Congress Catalog Card Number: 79–84891

First published in England by Weidenfeld & Nicolson

Designed by Michael Rand and Gilvrie Misstear

New York Graphic Society books are published by Little, Brown and
Company

Printed in England

Foreword
by John Hayes
Director of the
National Portrait Gallery

Of all forms of art, portraiture is one of the most elusive, and one of the most difficult for any artist effectively to master. This may well sound a paradoxical thing to say in view of the number of artists who practise it. But I think they would agree with me. It is partly that the human face, though of compelling interest to every one of us, remains the most mysterious of all subjects; and partly that, once an artist has achieved a likeness which he thinks credible, the pictorial means at his disposal – design, colour, line, associations – for amplifying that likeness, for defining the individuality of posture, gestures, movement, above all for revealing personality, are severely contained. It is not surprising that portraiture soon becomes trapped in formulae. For an example, one only has to look at the stock poses of the 17th or 18th centuries. Such formal limitations do not apply to anything like the same extent to landscape or to other genres.

But if this constriction is true of portrait painting – and how much more so of portrait sculpture – the case with portrait photography is worse, though different. Interpretation in this field cannot even begin with the virtues of a *tabula rasa*; the camera is only too well equipped, literally at the drop of a hat, to produce likeness – for the painter or the sculptor already a difficult skill. How can the photographer hope to escape the shackles of that inexorable image which lies within the confines of his lens, and ever begin to uncover personality? Arnold Newman has written that he is 'convinced that any photographic attempt to show the complete man is nonsense, to an extent. We can only show, as best we can, what the outer man reveals.' He is, however, relentlessly, and rightly, determined to interpret. In another place he writes that 'I became fascinated with the control of the camera and the ability to make it see as I saw.' Newman's control is legendary, and the vision he has imposed idiosyncratic, dependent upon exaggerations of one kind or another, dramatic close-ups, foreshortenings, perspectives. Deeply influenced by abstract painting and surrealism – it comes as no surprise to discover that his favourite painter is Mondrian – some of his photographs will date as surely as other derivative art. Others in this vein, such as his exquisite *Bridget Riley* (1966), fuse style and expressive portraiture with the apparent effortlessness of true genius, and will remain classic. Among compositions in which we are totally unconscious of manner, only of impeccable style, his *Harold Macmillan* (1954) and *Lyndon Johnson* (1963) are masterly, his *Marilyn Monroe* (1962) deeply sensitive, and the simple, massive nobility of his tribute to another great American photographer, Paul Strand (1966), breathtaking.

5

Arnold Newman is one of the giants of portrait photography, a subject in which he has specialized for over thirty years. We were, therefore, greatly honoured when he accepted our invitation and that of *The Sunday Times* to photograph a number of portraits of eminent British men and women especially for an exhibition to be held at the National Portrait Gallery. As an American he can look at the British dispassionately, or reasonably so. Detachment is an important element in portraiture. To be prejudiced, politically or socially, or to know too well, is often to start forgiving or excusing – or maligning. Not everyone is as relentless and accurate an observer as Rembrandt in his self-portraits.

Of course the title that was chosen, 'The Great British', is a misnomer. It ought to be 'Some Great Britons'. Many very distinguished people are not included. In the course of two comparatively short forays it was not possible for Mr Newman to photograph everyone we would have wished. Some people were not available, some were abroad. We were deeply grateful to him for enduring an exceptionally arduous programme; no less to George Perry and Christine Walker of *The Sunday Times* and to my colleague, Colin Ford, who were responsible for the organisation. Our most profound thanks, however, are due to Sir Denis Hamilton, Editor-in-Chief of Times Newspapers, who so generously agreed to sponsor this important undertaking and arrange for the publication of this book, and to Harold Evans, Editor of *The Sunday Times*, whose response to our initiative was characteristically enthusiastic. We also, and most warmly, thank the sitters who so kindly allowed themselves to be photographed, often at some inconvenience to themselves. The results, gathered together in this volume and discussed by Mr Perry in the Introduction which follows, are one of the Gallery's most significant recent accessions.

The National Portrait Gallery has been collecting photographs seriously only since 1968, the year of the Cecil Beaton exhibition. Now it is one of its principal activities; more and more photographs are being transferred from the archive to the main collection, and the importance of photography as a record will naturally increase as the years go by. It must be said that the Gallery is not concerned with photography as such. It is concerned with collecting the most vivid and penetrating likenesses of eminent British men and women in any media. In collecting images of the men and women of the past we often have to put up with the third-rate. No good portrait of Shakespeare exists. In the case of contemporary photographs there is no need for this. We can, and should, go out for the best. The Arnold Newman exhibition is indicative of the Gallery's new policy.

Introduction
by George Perry

Once the National Portrait Gallery had taken the decision to start a photographic collection, it was a logical step to invite a master photographer to make portraits of some of those English people whose achievements and eminence qualified them for inclusion in the Gallery. In 1976, Colin Ford, Keeper of Film and Photography, proposed that the NPG commission the American photographer Arnold Newman to do this but, for financial and other reasons, the project was not carried out. It might have stayed stillborn had it not been for Harold Evans, Editor of *The Sunday Times*. He was in New York in October 1977, and during research for his book on newspaper photography, *Pictures on a Page*,[1] met Arnold Newman. During the course of discussion, the project was mentioned. Without hesitation, Harold Evans told him that *The Sunday Times* would be happy to sponsor it, and to present the results to the National Portrait Gallery.

As soon as he returned to London he contacted the Gallery, and then assigned his staff to organise the practicalities. Not surprisingly it became a responsibility of *The Sunday Times Magazine*, which – with its high visual standards carefully maintained by its art director, Michael Rand – has securely established itself as one of Europe's leading platforms of photo-journalism. A high regard for the value of photography has been an important principle since its founding in 1962, and *The Sunday Times* during the twelve years of Harold Evans' editorship has done a great deal to heighten public appreciation of the historical and aesthetic importance, particularly in such campaigns as the acquisition by the National Portrait Gallery of three albums by D. O. Hill and Robert Adamson and the 'Herschel Album' of Julia Margaret Cameron's photographs, as well as the establishment by the Royal Photographic Society of its *Directory of British Photographic Collections*.[2]

To invite a giant of Arnold Newman's calibre to Britain in order to photograph seventy-five or so of the most celebrated people in the country for a major exhibition and for the permanent national collection seemed to us to be an unprecedented event. But as lists of possible sitters were worked out by *The Sunday Times* editors and the NPG staff an inevitable question arose from those who stood on the fringes of the project. Why had an American been honoured in this way, rather than an Englishman? Colin Ford's answer to this question is 'Quite simply, Arnold Newman is the best there is – for formal portraits, prepared, composed and executed with all the thoroughness and depth of an oil painting. He has shown the heights to which this kind of photography can rise'. We felt that the choice was entirely justified. Although

Lord Mountbatten is photographed at his home

Britain's place in the history of photography is of considerable magnitude, with such great Victorian trail-blazers as William Fox Talbot, David Octavius Hill and Robert Adamson, Julia Margaret Cameron and Roger Fenton making their mark, in our own times the camera is held in less esteem than in the United States, where it is of far greater consequence to the national culture. But British attitudes to photography have been changing in recent years.

There is, of course, nothing new in the work of a foreign artist appearing on the walls and in the archives of the National Portrait Gallery. No one could quibble at Holbein and Van Dyck. In more recent times, the 1969 painting of the Queen by Pietro Annigoni, which she herself is said to regard as her definitive portrait, has been one of its most popular acquisitions. It can be argued that the photographic portrait is inherently more valuable than the oil painting. The American critic Susan Sontag has noted that a photograph, being a registering of a light emanation, is in fact a material vestige of its subject in a way that no painting can be:

'Between two fantasy alternatives, that Holbein the Younger had lived long enough to have painted Shakespeare or that a prototype of the camera had been invented early enough to have photographed him, most Bardolators would choose the photograph. This is not just because it would presumably show what Shakespeare really looked like, for even if the hypothetical photograph were faded, barely legible, a brownish shadow, we would probably still prefer it to another glorious Holbein. Having a photograph of Shakespeare would be like having a nail from the True Cross.'[3]

Her statement does not, of course, invalidate the painting, but it does recognise the uniqueness of the photographic record, and its special authenticity of revelation that cannot be matched by the artist's brush.

It is easy enough for anyone to step into an automatic photographic booth, slip a couple of coins into a slot and pose for a quartet of miniature portraits of an order that would satisfy the Passport Office. Some of the official record photography has hitherto been of an order of imagination on much the same level. Therefore the foresight of the National Portrait Gallery in seeking a photographic register of the men and women who make our times as seen by the best living photographers must be highly commended.

That Arnold Newman belongs to that select group cannot be disputed. He trained as a painter but sees his work also as journalism. He approaches his subjects with a sense of history, a need to show them as they were on that particular day in their lives, and yet there is a great difference in method between him and what one normally imagines a photo-journalist to be – shooting from the hip, seizing the moment. An Arnold Newman photograph is a finely-honed demon-

Arnold Newman working in David Hockney's studio

Nobel prizewinners are posed in the
Wren Library at Trinity College, Cambridge

stration of control, each detail considered and calculated, polished to perfection. There is also a rare and potent imagination that gives his pictures a vibrant force – there is nothing sterile or lifeless about them.

He is a restless perfectionist, edgy and nervous when he is preparing to shoot. He is burly, bearded, smokes cigars as a connoisseur, and occasionally wears a beret when he is working. He was born in New York on 3 March 1918, of middle-class Jewish parentage. During the Twenties his father underwent various financial crises, culminating in the 1929 crash which destroyed his dry goods concern. After that he went into the hotel leasing business, and the family divided their life between Atlantic City, New Jersey, in the summer, and Miami Beach, Florida, in the winter. By the age of 12 young Arnold was showing immense promise in art, and was given constant encouragement by his parents. After graduating from high school he was offered an art scholarship at the University of Miami, Coral Gables, which required him to perform a multiplicity of jobs such as hiring models and painting scenery as well as studying. He was there from 1936 until 1938, when he was forced to leave through lack of funds. He then found a job through a family friend as an apprentice in a Philadelphia photographic studio. He immediately showed a remarkable capacity to learn the craft of photography. It was exacting work – the studio was a department store concession, and he would often have to photograph seventy sitters in one day, but after hours he would experiment with his own photography, and explore the mysteries of the darkroom. He abandoned his former ambition of being a painter, and dedicated himself to his new calling. In December 1939 he became manager of a studio, part of a chain, in West Palm Beach, Florida, at twice the salary, enabling him to buy a large format, view camera. Newman's greatest influence at the time was Walker Evans, and many early photographs show how assiduously he had grasped his idol's manner and technique. It was his hope to work like Evans for the Farm Security Administration under Roy Stryker, yet by the time he met Stryker in 1941 it was disbanding as America turned to thoughts of war.

But by now he had met Beaumont Newhall, then Curator of Photography at the Museum of Modern Art in New York, who urged him to show his work to another of his idols, the great photographer and gallery dealer, Alfred Stieglitz. Then followed a joint show with Ben Rose at the A–D Gallery, which was favourably received by the critics, and Newhall purchased for the Museum the first of many Arnold Newman photographs. Heartened by the success he decided to move permanently to New York and become a fully-fledged professional photographer. He became acquainted with many of the artists in New York at that time, an exciting milieu enriched by such refugees from Europe as Léger, Mondrian, Grosz and Chagall, and enjoyed photographing them in their surroundings.

In the autumn of 1942 he returned to Florida to enter military service, but was temporarily deferred. For the rest of the war he ran a portrait studio in Miami Beach that eventually employed nine photographers and assistants. On visits to New York he continued to photograph painters and sculptors, and in 1945 he had his first one man show, at the Philadelphia Museum of Art, called *Artists Look Like This*. It gave him the impetus to abandon the profitable studio and to take a chance in New York as a freelance. He moved back there in 1946 and soon afterwards received his first *Life* assignment, a portrait of Eugene O'Neill. He also took his first, and his most famous photograph of Stravinsky, in which the lid of a grand piano fills most of the frame, and which ironically was rejected at the time by *Harper's Bazaar*, who had commissioned it. He moved into a studio apartment on West Sixty-Seventh Street, which remained as his photographic base, although since the mid-Fifties his residence has been an even more handsome studio apartment two doors away, its walls studded with an exquisite art collection, much of which was received over the years in exchange for photographic prints of their originators.

In 1948 he met Augusta Rubinstein, who was working for Teddy Kollek in New York, surreptitiously smuggling arms to Israel for the Haganah. They married and later had two sons, Eric and David, now respectively a neuro-biologist and architect. Augusta Newman is the cornerstone of Arnold Newman's personal and business life, for not only has she raised their sons, but she is his studio manager and business associate. In the years that have passed an astonishing parade of celebrity and genius has come before his lens. There is scarcely, it would seem, any figure of cultural importance in America who has not sat for Arnold Newman. Every president since Truman has been photographed and so have political leaders in many other countries. Quite often the Newman portrait is regarded as the definitive image, and the public at large, who might have difficulty in naming the photographer, would certainly instantly recognise the picture. Through his work in such magazines as *Life*, *Fortune*, *Harper's Bazaar*, *Holiday* and *Look* he has reached a wide audience, and he has also worked extensively in advertising and on various books. He has had many exhibitions, including a major retrospective in 1972 at the George Eastman House, Rochester, N.Y., and in 1974 a collection of 150

Above: Henry Moore is photographed in his studio at Much Hadham, Herts. Below: a close-up is made of a drawing of hands. Right: the resulting photograph

portraits was published under the title *One Mind's Eye*.[3]

The book is used by Arnold Newman as an aid towards getting the kind of pictures he wants. Invariably he will have a copy among his items of equipment, and if his sitters are unfamiliar with it, he will produce it and give them a chance to browse. They will look at the studies of Picasso and Braque, Ben-Gurion and John F. Kennedy and should sense what Newman is after. Few can feel unflattered at joining such company.

The National Portrait Gallery laid down the criteria by which potential sitters were selected. They looked to the future, say fifty years hence, and asked, would these names still mean something? The fact that the storerooms are stuffed with paintings of long-forgotten Victorian and Edwardian notables testifies to the fallibility of this kind of assessment, which eventually must rest on the subjective judgement of those making the choice. It is a broad list, occasionally controversial, and perhaps weighted on the side of maturity and wisdom rather than youthful promise.

Most of the pictures were taken over a six-week period in the late spring of 1978. Christine Walker, a researcher at *The Sunday Times*, performed the delicate and complex task of dovetailing all the appointments into the calendar, allowing sufficient time to travel, set up the shot and shoot. Scarcely anyone who received an invitation declined. The few who did were mostly abroad or in ill health. But an attempt to make a group of the seven editors of Fleet Street's quality daily and Sunday papers foundered when the editor of *The Times* felt that for them to be seen collectively would go against their general interests.

The first stage would be for Christine Walker to prepare a brief on the subject's career from cuttings in *The Sunday Times* library. As some had achieved their fame and reputation solely on this side of the Atlantic they were unfamiliar to Arnold Newman, and as a guide to how he interpreted them in their photographs he needed to know where they fitted in to the spectrum of British life. There would then follow the question of location. The setting is fundamental to the Newman style, for it is the environment in which a subject is placed that reflects and reveals his essence. Wherever possible the place chosen would be where the sitter worked, be it studio or study, library or office. In some cases it was necessary for the setting to be symbolic, either to preserve impartiality in the group subjects (Cambridge Nobel prizewinners in the Wren Library at Trinity; Oxford Regius Professors in the Library of Christ Church; London publishers at the National Book League) or for the simpler reason that it produced an interesting picture.

New York selection time. (L to R) George Perry, editor, Arnold Newman, Michael Rand, art director

Reminder for Mr Callaghan in the Cabinet Room

During a location reconnaissance at the Royal Opera House for the shot of Sir Frederick Ashton we stumbled on the Floral Hall, a beautiful glass-roofed structure with cast-iron columns and ornamental bosses, which since the disappearance of the Covent Garden market had become a temporary storehouse for scenery. Not only were there limitless photographic possibilities, with its constantly changing props – one day a twelve-foot-high fireplace, the next a rustic hillside made of plaster – but the natural light filtering through the roof lights was exciting. Eventually, three very disparate pictures were shot there – Morecambe and Wise against a no-seam backdrop, Sir Geraint Evans, and the trio of actresses, Susannah York, Susan Hampshire and Judi Dench, the last using the space to great effect.

In some instances the locations had a special significance. Lord Denning had never before been photographed in his own court in his robes as Master of the Rolls. Lord Home sought permission for a shot in the Royal Gallery at the House of Lords (Arnold Newman, used to the way former American chief executives might assert themselves, was amazed that an ex-Prime Minister could not just do as he wished, but was as punctilious at observing the proper procedure as the humblest backbench MP) and Edward Heath was photographed in St Stephen's Hall, with occasional interruptions when a Member walked through the shot as if to demonstrate that a privilege was being granted. It was particularly fortunate that the Royal Albert Hall had a spare afternoon when Sir William Walton was making one of his rare visits to London. To have rented such a location would have cost a sum running into thousands, but the management was delighted to give Sir William its freedom.

The Sunday Times used the Kensington flat of Mrs Susan Barnes Crosland, widow of the late Foreign Secretary, Anthony Crosland, for Arnold Newman and his wife during the period of principal shooting. The first arrival at the flat on the morning of a shoot would be Chris Nation, who had been engaged as Arnold Newman's assistant. His calm, level-headed and thorough approach proved to be of tremendous value. On days when a particularly complex session was expected, a second assistant, George Hewitt, would also attend. Next to arrive would be the researcher, Christine Walker, and then the Senior Editor (myself), or someone deputed by me to be present to ensure all went smoothly. Such was the interest in the project on *The Sunday Times Magazine* that several colleagues were anxious to see Arnold Newman at work, and so when appropriate subjects came up they were invited to attend and assist with their special knowledge. Thus Tony Osman, the Science Editor, smoothed the way for the shot of the Cambridge scientists, and Bruce Bernard, the Picture Editor, who in a chequered youth had worked backstage at the Royal Opera House, helped to organise the Ashton shot. Colin Ford at the National Portrait Gallery shouldered the task of getting eight Regius Professors into the same room at the same time.

When several boxes of equipment had been loaded into what had become an impossibly small estate car the party would set off for the location, arriving at least an hour and often earlier before shooting was due to start. In spite of his eagerness to allow plenty of time Arnold Newman invariably knew the shot that he wanted to do within two minutes of his arrival. Time would still be needed to set up lights and make Polaroids to check colour exposure, using whoever happened to be around as a stand-in for the sitter. A doorman might suddenly find himself playing an archbishop. Should the sitter arrive early while preparations were still going on, he too might find himself used for the test shots, but Newman always preferred to solve his problems in advance and spare the subject an additional ordeal.

Part of his skill resides in an ability to put the subject at ease before shooting. There is much small talk, which is nevertheless pertinent. For it enables Newman to make assessments of the sitter's capacity to unstiffen, respond and help to produce a good photograph. His manner has an engaging, almost bumbling aspect which elicits a friendly, sympathetic response, but also masks a ruthless desire for perfection. He shoots a lot of film, and sometimes a session only begins to work after many exposures. 'Film is the cheapest thing I've got,' he will say as another 35mm cassette is dropped out of the camera. He works with Nikon 35mm SLRs, and also with a Hasselblad. But his joy is his 5 × 4 view camera with which he can correct converging verticals and achieve a sumptuous depth and resolution. He likes to stop down to a narrow aperture and to use natural, or available light as much as possible, which often means that exposures are long, requiring considerable stamina by the sitter. He will work all around a gesture or expression he is seeking, squeezing off innumerable shots, with increasing excitement until he suddenly realises that he has it, when he will cry 'Don't move – hold it! One more! And another!' as he tries to get as many shots as he can before the moment vanishes. He confesses to Walter Mitty-ish feelings when confronted with heads of state, that he should be in a position to tell them what to do and that they should do it.

Taking the picture, as every photographer will aver, is but one part of the operation. The great test that follows is in the darkroom. The contacts, and there may be several sheets of

Arnold Newman at his alma mater, the University of Miami, at work photographing Dr Francis Crick

Arnold Newman, Chris Bonington and researcher
Christine Walker on location in Cumbrian hills

them, must be scrutinised through a glass very carefully. Promising shots are marked for printing, and literally dozens of test prints will be made until he is satisfied that he has the right quality. Among the thousands of dollars-worth of sophisticated equipment in Arnold Newman's studio are two L-shaped pieces of cardboard. Yet they are one of his most essential accessories. He pushes them across a print to indicate the crop, how the picture is to be masked. Many of his most stunning effects have been achieved by imaginative cropping. No art director can dare to impose his crop on a Newman picture. There can only be one crop, that made by Newman himself, for it is an integral part of the picture.

An Arnold Newman photograph is something, therefore, that is produced with immense care. Much of his creativity is spent in the darkroom, printing, bleaching, coaxing an immaculate print into existence with the finesse of a master craftsman. Each is a 'one-off' – there are no assembly line clones. The finished print is the summation of his skills at composing the picture, selecting the image, cropping and printing it. One of his frequent sayings is that a good portrait must first of all be a good photograph, and for that he strives. But what he insists that the public judge is not the technical expertise that lies behind the successful photograph – such a concern would be as arid as a discussion on the types of brushes and pigments used by Turner, a not invalid topic for an obsessive enthusiast, yet unnecessary as a basis on which to judge the picture – but the effect the image has when it is looked at, preferably on a wall in a gallery, like a painting, or at least reproduced by the best possible methods.

That Arnold Newman trained as a painter is apparent in his photographs, in his ordered sense of composition. Sometimes his subjects seem almost submerged by it, elements in a dazzling design. When he photographs an artist he often seems to be deliberately echoing their work with the camera, not as parody but as homage. He has found a visual way of saying 'Le style est l'homme'. Francis Bacon, toplit by a stark light bulb, almost becomes one of his own tortured figures, while the pose of Sir Cecil Beaton is quintessentially him and unmistakable. Beaton and Bill Brandt, as the two greatest living masters of British photography, were included as a special tribute by Arnold Newman, as were the trio of Duffy, Donovan and Bailey who electrified Sixties' attitudes.

Often Newman pictures become abstractions, with geometric shapes interconnecting with each other – the bold triangles created by parts of aircraft in the Laker picture, the placing of the open manuscript in the Tippett shot. That which seems casual may have been carefully arranged to make the mood – the sloping rows of books in Betjeman and

Pope-Hennessy, the three chairs behind Dame Marie Rambert balancing the divisions created by the *barre* supports to the left. A wall and pillar can become theatrical flats, as in the Hall-Nunn picture, or open scores on orchestra stands can float away from the beholder like the rippling notes of Walton's music. The starkness of some of the lines in his compositions are reminiscent of Mondrian, and he perhaps more than any other artist taught Newman the strengths and subtleties that could be found in geometric design. That he had a receptive pupil is demonstrated in an Arnold Newman story. He tells of how when he was in his early twenties he saw Mondrian in his studio in New York, working on one of his studies of intersecting lines. He asked Newman's opinion and the brash youth said that he thought one of the lines should be an eighth of an inch further over. Mondrian looked at his canvas again and said he was right, and went ahead and made the change.

The bulk of the photographs comprising *The Great British* were made after Arnold Newman had turned 60. The exceptions were the shot of Francis Bacon, taken two years earlier and included because he felt that he could make no better statement of how he saw him, and the three photographers, shot when Arnold Newman was lecturing at the Royal Photographic Society on a visit prior to the start of the series. Sir John Pope-Hennessy was photographed in his New York home, almost on Newman's doorstep, while Francis Crick was taken in Miami, a hometown of youth.

By his nature Arnold Newman is restless, creative and charged. His work programme has horrified younger men, and he is at his best when the adrenalin is flowing strongly. He strongly resents the occasional reminders that he has reached late middle age, and does not easily tolerate infirmities. 'I now have more ideas about photography,' he declares, 'there are more things that I wish to explore, and I feel more alive, than I did thirty years ago, when I was half my age. Young people may have more spontaneity. We have a saying in America – the pitcher is beginning to pitch with his head instead of his arm. But a creative person, if he keeps his mind alive, can still have strength in his arm. Look at Stravinsky, Picasso, both of whom I knew, and any number of writers who did such great things in later life. A creative medium gives you the chance to be alive.'

1 *Pictures on a Page: Photo-journalism, Graphics and Picture Editing.* Harold Evans. Heinemann, London 1978.
2 *Directory of British Photographic Collections.* Compiled by John Wall. Heinemann, London 1977.
3 *On Photography.* Susan Sontag. Allen Lane, London 1978.
4 *One Mind's Eye.* The Portraits and other photographs of Arnold Newman. David R. Godine, Boston 1974. New York Graphic Society, Boston 1978.

The end of the Morecambe and Wise session

The Photographs

'Of all the great actors of our time I think he is the most capable of submerging his own personality and becoming someone else. The instant my camera came out he found it difficult to be himself and was very shy and self-conscious. But soon we began to warm up and at the very end I was getting the pictures I had been seeking. Don't forget that I was photographing Guinness, the man who happens also to be an actor, rather than Guinness playing a part. That would have been much easier.'

Alec Guinness was born in 1914 in London and on leaving school went into advertising as a copywriter. In 1933 he turned to acting, and played a modern dress Hamlet at the Old Vic in 1938. After wartime naval service he returned to the Old Vic and also began a brilliant film career with 'Great Expectations' followed by a series of Ealing films, and 'The Bridge on the River Kwai' for which he won an Oscar. His stage career has included many great performances, both in classical and modern works such as 'The Cocktail Party', 'A Voyage Round My Father', and 'The Old Country'. He was knighted in 1959.

1 **Sir Alec Guinness. Actor. Queen's Theatre, London**

'She's as well known in America as she is in England. She's an extraordinary youthful, vivacious woman. The big surprise was that her offices and workrooms which melt together are small in size and resemble a rabbit warren. There was a small amount of re-arranging – we added a few things to the pinboard, bringing a number of ideas together. I believe that I captured a pixieish quality I was not too surprised to find in her.'

Mary Quant is Director of a company group bearing her name, and is an internationally-acclaimed fashion designer and innovator. She trained at Goldsmiths' College, London, and started her first company in 1955. A winner of many design awards, she was more instrumental than anyone in propagating the 'London look' of the Sixties, the era of the miniskirt. In recent years she has entered the cosmetic field with flair and success. She received an OBE in 1966, and an exhibition, 'Mary Quant's London', was staged by the London Museum in 1973.

2 Mary Quant.   Fashion designer and director.   Chelsea, London

'Lord Clark lives in a house in the grounds of Saltwood Castle, but still often works in the large library. We drove over to look at it with him. As we entered the drive a vintage Bentley suddenly appeared coming at us head-on at enormous speed. At the last second it skidded up on the bank and stopped inches from us. I must say that Lord Clark was rather cool about the whole thing and without turning a hair said of the other driver "Good Lord – he's nearly killed his grandfather!" I silently said to myself "And me!" The room we photographed in was very exciting, but it was dark, gloomy and cold and the weather had turned to heavy rain, some of which was coming through the ceiling. The picture was taken almost entirely with available light. We used reflectors and white sheets with light bouncing off, but the contrast was so great we could only get what I wanted with a great deal of effort.'

As Kenneth Clark he has received world fame for his elegantly produced series 'Civilisation', made in 1969. As an art historian he has conveyed his taste and scholarship to many millions. He was born in 1903, educated at Winchester and Trinity College, Oxford. From 1934 to 1945 he was Director of the National Gallery, Slade Professor of Fine Art at Oxford 1946–50 and 1961–2, Chairman of the Arts Council 1953–60, Chairman of Independent Television 1954–7. His many books include definitive studies of Leonardo, landscape painting, the nude in art, Rembrandt and the drawings of Henry Moore. He became a Life Peer in 1969 and received the Order of Merit in 1976.

3 Lord Clark, OM, CH.   Art historian.   Saltwood, Hythe, Kent

'She was one of the most incredible women I have ever met. At over 90 she was even able to work a little at the *barre*, and as everybody knows, was so full of spirit as to make the rest of us at middle age look like old fogies. I photographed her in her studio, her workshop. I was looking for a framework for this very spirited lady, who sat there and was very amused at the way I went about taking pictures. I was very aware of the way she, as a dancer and choreographer, positioned her body and hands.'

Marie Rambert was born in Warsaw in 1888 and was a member of Diaghilev's Ballets Russes 1912–13. She married the British playwright Ashley Dukes in 1918 and opened the Rambert Ballet School in 1920. The Ballet Rambert was founded in 1926. For more than fifty years she has been an extraordinary force in British ballet, and her contribution is unrivalled, many brilliant dancers owing their careers to her. She was made a Dame of the British Empire in 1962.

**4   Dame Marie Rambert.
Founder Ballet Rambert.   Chiswick, London**

'This picture was taken on the same day that the England team was departing for Australia. Consequently, there was a certain amount of pressure as there were news photographers waiting to get close to Boycott, who had been involved in considerable controversy with the Yorkshire Cricket Club that very day, and had arrived late from Leeds owing to a delayed train. I found myself in the midst of turmoil and conditions were not ideal. Boycott was tremendously helpful, though. I decided to go for an abstraction as I was not allowed to take a picture on the Lord's pitch, but I was permitted to use the Nursery grounds. The only way that I could photograph him was to come in very tight and to use the elements of hand, cap and bat to say what he is without being too literal. I think that it works as a powerful image.'

Geoffrey Boycott was born in 1940. He is one of the most dedicated batsmen in cricketing history, although his career for Yorkshire and England has been controversial. His highest score in test cricket was 246 not out in 1967 against India. He became Captain of Yorkshire in 1971, when he became the first English batsman to average 100 in a first class season.

5 **Geoffrey Boycott. Cricketer. Lord's, London**

'For various reasons we ruled out photographing him in costume because he would then be too specifically identified with an operatic character. But with his flair and way of flinging his coat around his shoulders he made it appear almost like an operatic costume. There is something very flamboyant about the gesture. It was a very enjoyable session in what had become my favourite London "studio", the Floral Hall adjoining the Royal Opera House.'

Geraint Evans, principal baritone at the Royal Opera House, was born in 1922, and received his musical education at the Guildhall School. His ROH career began in 1948, and he has performed at most of the world's great opera houses. His most famous role is Falstaff. He was knighted in 1969.

6 Sir Geraint Evans.   Singer.   Covent Garden, London

'We had to get into St Stephen's Hall long before the public arrived. This picture was a re-shoot, the first not being at all to my liking. Mr Heath, although like myself not a morning man, showed up at an early hour just to make sure that we had a successful photograph. The portrait is very much a reflection of his personality. I felt that the great Victorian neo-Gothic interior of the Palace of Westminster was the perfect symbolic background for the former Prime Minister.'

Edward Heath was born at Broadstairs in 1916, educated at Chatham House, Ramsgate, and Balliol College, Oxford, where he was President of the Union. After war service in the army he became prospective Conservative candidate for Bexley, winning the seat in the 1950 election. In 1965 he became leader of the party and from 1970 to 1974 was Prime Minister. He was the chief architect of Britain's entry into Europe. Aside from politics his over-riding passions are music and sailing, both of which he embraces with perfectionist skill, and in 1971 he captained Britain's winning Admiral's Cup Team.

7 **Rt Hon Edward Heath.   Prime Minister 1970–74.   Westminster, London**

'I knew Bill from earlier visits. I have great awe of his photographic genius and have been influenced by him. I knew his apartment reflected his personality and I knew exactly what I wanted to do. He has a superficial frailty that makes you sympathetic. It is only gradually that you realise that the inner strength of this man is steel, which enables him to make his immensely strong photographs. Incidentally, Polacolor represents flesh tones best when it is used with strobe, and not with natural light. I re-created daylight by putting sheets where the windows were and bounced the strobes to get the exact kind of colour that I wanted.'

Bill Brandt was born in 1904 and spent much of his early youth in Switzerland and Germany. He studied with Man Ray in Paris in the Thirties, and at the age of 25 became a photo-journalist. He developed a distinctive style of social documentary reportage, using contrasty texture and shadow. He turned to photographing nudes in the Forties, often placing them in landscapes to form abstract shapes. The Museum of Modern Art, New York honoured him with an exhibition in 1969, which came to the Hayward Gallery, London in 1970.

Bill Brandt.   Photographer. Hampstead, London

Susannah York, Susan Hampshire, Judi Dench. Actresses. Covent Garden, London

'It was fun to find these fine actresses as they really were. I decided strongly against photographing them in *Vogue*-type elegance, and they all came as modern women with attractive life-styles – Susan Hampshire, the wife of a prime minister in *The Pallisers*, even turning up on the back of a motor bike! So I decided to keep them in their street clothes. Once again I used my favourite London "studio" – the Floral Hall. I went back to the old photographer's cliché, no-seam paper, but used it to emphasise the reality around them. By isolating the setting against the real surroundings, and using exaggerated poses we were all poking gentle fun at the theatricality of it all.'

Judi Dench was born in 1934, educated at The Mount, York, and the Central School of Speech and Drama. She has appeared in several films and won an award for her television part in 'Talking to a Stranger', but stage performances in roles as varied as Lady Macbeth for the Royal Shakespeare Company and Sally Bowles in 'Cabaret' have established her. She received the OBE in 1970.

Susan Hampshire was born in 1942 and educated at her parents' school in Knightsbridge, London. Since her debut in 'Expresso Bongo' she has appeared in many plays and films, but her best-known roles have been those in such long-running TV epics as 'The Forsyte Saga' and 'The Pallisers'.

Susannah York was born in London in 1941 and studied at the Royal Academy of Dramatic Art. Her first film was 'Tunes of Glory' in 1960. She has since played in many films in Britain and America, including 'Tom Jones', 'The Battle of Britain', 'They Shoot Horses, Don't They?' and 'Superman'.

'Powell's Belgravia home was surprisingly modest, but comfortable. His study was appropriate for a very active political figure. In America we know a great deal about him, but I was still surprised by his tremendous intensity, something I wanted to capture. When he greeted us he was dictating to his secretary in his carpet slippers. He insisted on going to put his boots on, although I told him it was not really necessary as I was only photographing his head and shoulders. "Ah," he said, "a man is not himself until he has his boots on!" – a remark that I thought was most telling. His small room with its highly organised clutter also reflected his personality, and everything was precise and in its proper place.'

Enoch Powell, born 1912, was educated at King Edward's, Birmingham, and Trinity College, Cambridge. He was Professor of Greek at the University of Sydney 1937–9 and during the war rose from private to brigadier. In 1950 he became Conservative Member of Parliament for Wolverhampton SW and served in the Government as Financial Secretary to the Treasury and Minister of Health. Notorious for his maverick views on such topics as the Common Market and immigration, he resigned the party whip and was re-elected as Ulster Unionist MP for South Down in 1974.

10 Rt Hon Enoch Powell.   Politician.   South Eaton Place, London

'Due to the tremendous pressures on both these men, it was hard to find the right time – it eventually turned out to be 8 a.m. – to get them together, and to find a neutral background. Unhappily, the very short time set aside by Trevor Nunn was cut even further by a television demand. I'm frankly startled that I got a good photograph out of it. The immense pillars, suggesting stage flats, are part of the structure of the Barbican development. Peter Hall lives there, and Trevor Nunn's new theatre is being built on the site.'

Born at Bury St Edmund's in 1930 and educated at the Perse School and Pembroke College, Cambridge, Peter Hall became Director of the Royal Shakespeare Theatre in 1960 and masterminded the RSC as a separate permanent ensemble. In 1973 he became Director of the National Theatre, and was knighted in 1977.

Trevor Nunn was born in 1940, educated at Northgate Grammar School, Ipswich, and Downing College, Cambridge, and since 1968 has been Artistic Director of the Royal Shakespeare Company.

11 Sir Peter Hall, Trevor Nunn. Theatre directors. Barbican, London

'All offices are difficult to photograph in. I looked all over the TUC seeking a suitable setting other than his office. Finally I entered it and found that the picture had been waiting for me all along. The piles of papers, letters, notes and the rest on his desk were the perfect abstract foil for the man himself. He was working in his shirtsleeves when I arrived, and I asked him to stay like that for the photograph. The knick-knacks and memorabilia in his office startled me, for a short while earlier I had photographed a union chief in Chicago, and the two offices were almost interchangeable.'

Len Murray, General Secretary of the Trades Union Congress since 1973, was born in 1922, educated at Wellington Grammar School, Salop, the University of London and New College, Oxford. He joined the Economic Department of the TUC in 1947 and was head of the department 1954–69. He was made a Privy Councillor in 1976.

12   Rt Hon Lionel Murray.   General Secretary, Trades Union Congress.   Bloomsbury, London

'Lord Grade was everything I had heard – expansive, flamboyant, warm – and in contrast to so many other entertainment tycoons a man I felt I could trust! The most difficult cliché to overcome is the man behind the desk, but this time the desk, walls, pictures and memorabilia were the reflection of the man himself. It took the minimum time to make this portrait.'

Lew Grade was once one half of a music hall act with his brother Leslie. He was born in 1906, and has been in the entertainment business all his working life. His interests include ATV, Moss Empires, Pye Records and ITC. He is a prominent international film producer, and was responsible for 'Capricorn One' and 'The Muppet Movie'. He was knighted in 1969 and made a Life Peer in 1976. He chose to be known as Lord Grade of Elstree, after one of the homes of the British film and television industry.

13　Lord Grade.　Company chairman.　Great Cumberland Place, London

'It was difficult to believe that he had been a war hero – he was shy, gentle and physically slight. His enthusiasm ran through his work. What impressed me was his introspective nature. Given a few moments of quiet he had a tendency to turn inward quite a bit. I began to recognise the goodness and dedication of this man. To me this is an impressionistic photograph. The image above him, of a blind woman in South Africa, breaks the quietness. The simplicity of the photograph reflects the austere way in which Cheshire and his wife live.'

Leonard Cheshire was born in 1917, educated at Stowe and Merton College, Oxford. He joined the Royal Air Force in 1939 and won the DSO (with two bars), the DFC and in 1944 the VC. In 1945 he was the official British observer of the dropping of an atomic bomb on Nagasaki. After the war he founded the Cheshire Foundation Homes. There are now 140 homes for the disabled in 35 countries. In 1959 he married Sue Ryder.

14   Group Captain Leonard Cheshire.   Founder of homes for the disabled.   Cavendish, Suffolk

'He was a delight, full of humour, and understood exactly what I had in mind. This was one case where the photograph was deliberately theatrical. There's an area above the stage at the Royal Opera House, Covent Garden, where they paint the scenery. When I walked in, to my delight there were these huge, unpainted flats which were perfect, for they echoed the kind of abstract and simple backgrounds so frequently used in ballet. The greatest difficulty was that the whole area was lit by just a dim skylight, so I needed exposures of two or three seconds in length. I got them from Sir Frederick without any movement from him.'

Frederick Ashton was born in Ecuador in 1904, and educated by the Dominican Fathers, Lima, Peru, and at Dover College. He was Founder-choreographer to the Royal Ballet (Principal Choreographer 1933–70 and Director 1963–70) and among his successful ballets are 'Les Patineurs', 'Symphonic Variations', 'Facade', 'Romeo and Juliet' and 'Cinderella'. He was knighted in 1962 and made a Companion of Honour in 1970.

15 **Sir Frederick Ashton, CH.   Choreographer.   Covent Garden, London**

'I did this portrait of Bacon in London in 1975. When it was agreed that he would be among "The Great British" I felt that it would be impossible to improve upon it. I think that it is one of my best from any period. It was partially planned, partially an accident. While I was working in his studio getting him into position he moved under the light. I said "Please stay there!" and quickly made my exposure. I feel that it reflects subconsciously the horrors and distortions of his work, even the skylight echoes the box-like structure of many of his paintings. I didn't look for it, it just happened to appear in a way that astonished me, particularly the reflection of the bulb in the ceiling and the twisted wire. An art critic in New York felt that the picture was too planned. It was one of the least planned pictures that I have ever taken, but probably one of the best discoveries.'

Francis Bacon was born in Dublin in 1909. He is one of the most important and influential painters in Europe. Since his first one-man show at the Hanover Gallery in 1949 he has dominated the British art world. His work is strong, anguished and uncompromising, exerting a powerful emotional effect on the viewer. His most famous painting is probably 'Study after Velasquez's portrait of Pope Innocent X', first shown in 1953.

16 Francis Bacon.   Artist.   Kensington, London

'The picture was taken at Sir Harold's country home, in the old adjoining barn which has been converted into his workroom. It seemed very fitting as a study for an ex-Prime Minister. One thing that amused us was a desk lamp presented by an admiring constituent showing such places as the Houses of Parliament and Number Ten, which went from day to night when the light came on. The choice of the pipe was as much his as mine. He said he always felt much more comfortable with the pipe in his hand rather than in his pocket, where it produced an awkward bulge. With anybody but Sir Harold the pipe and the dog would have been gross clichés.'

Harold Wilson was born in Huddersfield in 1916, was educated at Wirral Grammar School and Jesus College, Oxford, and entered Parliament in 1945 after a wartime Civil Service career. He was President of the Board of Trade in the Attlee Government until 1951, and succeeded Hugh Gaitskell as leader of the Labour Party in 1963. He was Prime Minister from 1964 until 1970, and 1974–6. He was knighted when he resigned that office.

Rt Hon Sir Harold Wilson.   Prime Minister 1964–70, 1974–6. Great Missenden, Bucks

Lord Denning.   Master of the Rolls. Law Courts, London

'I wanted to photograph the Master of the Rolls in his own court. Lord Denning said "What a marvellous idea! Why hasn't anyone thought of that before?" He was obviously delighted with the concept. On the day I had problems with the light, as black rain clouds gathered outside. I was forced to create more and more artificial daylight as we went along. I hope, for all that, it is still a good photograph.'

Lord Denning, Master of the Rolls since 1962, is Britain's senior judge, and is regarded as the greatest living expert in English jurisprudence. He was born in 1899, educated at Andover Grammar School and Magdalen College, Oxford. Called to the Bar in 1923 he became a KC in 1938, Judge of the High Court in 1944, Lord Justice of Appeal 1948–57, Lord of Appeal 1957–62.

'The picture coincided with the London opening of *Evita*. The night before I had gone to the first preview, made notes and decided my attitude. I was particularly struck by the fabulous staging, and decided to make use of the stark simplicity of the lighting and rather theatrical use of the black stage. I wanted two men of the theatre interacting with each other. Lloyd Webber, the composer, was tremendously preoccupied with the audience reaction and possible changes he might make to the score. I was able to move him like a zombie from place to place. It was only when I was able to shoot that he came alive and was aware of the camera. Rice, the lyricist, was rather amused by this and everything else, being greatly relieved by the audience reaction the previous night. It was just as well – if it had been bad I don't know what kind of a picture I would have gotten. The stage was lit from underneath by aircraft landing lights which were excessively hot, and only supposed to be put on for short periods. I left them on too long and black smoke suddenly began to fill the stage. Had we not quickly turned them off *Evita* might have ended before it began!'

Andrew Lloyd Webber was born in 1948, and educated at Westminster School. Apart from the musicals he has composed in collaboration with Tim Rice, he was responsible for the stage musical 'Jeeves' and various film scores.

Tim Rice, born in 1944, was educated at Lancing. Initially he worked in the record industry, but in 1968 collaborated with Andrew Lloyd Webber to write the lyrics for 'Joseph and the Amazing Technicolor Dreamcoat', followed by 'Jesus Christ Superstar' and 'Evita'.

19 Tim Rice, Andrew Lloyd Webber.   Lyricist, composer.   Prince Edward Theatre, London

'This was the very first photograph specifically for "The Great British". It was taken on my homeground – Sir John has an apartment on New York's East Side. His study was a marvellous clutter, a very real workroom. Some of the pictures I took were more formal, but I found this one which looked to me rather quizzical represents what he is about – his quizzical attitude towards art and his work in general. Although the picture may look casual it is very carefully structured. I used the wide-angle lens especially to encompass the papers, the books and the reflection of the books at the rear. None of this is an accident.'

Sir John Pope-Hennessy is Consultative Chairman of European Paintings at the Metropolitan Museum, New York, and Professor of Fine Arts at New York University, holding both posts since 1977. Before that he was Director of the Victoria and Albert Museum 1967–73, and of the British Museum 1974–6. He was born in 1913 and educated at Downside and Balliol. He is one of the world's greatest authorities on the Italian Renaissance period and author of many standard works on its related subjects.

20   Sir John Pope-Hennessy.   Art historian.   Park Avenue, New York

'His face and ebullient personality are very well known in America through his television commercials. The day started off beautifully, and I planned my pictures taking into account the sunlight and the contrast that came from that. However, after we had chosen our location, a typical English gloom spread across Gatwick Airport and remained there all the time I was taking my photograph. Our biggest problem was that a cold wind sprang up, making it difficult for Sir Freddie to hold still and prevent his hair from blowing about. As usual, he was in great humour and great spirit. I felt that the usual corporate image, boardroom approach was definitely not for him.'

Born in 1922, Freddie Laker was educated at the Simon Langton School, Canterbury, and worked as an apprentice at Shorts, Rochester. During the war he served with the Air Transport Auxiliary, and afterwards founded an airline (Aviation Traders) from war surplus aircraft. In 1960 he started British United Airways, and was instrumental in getting the BAC 1–11 into the air. In 1966 he formed Laker Airways and fought relentlessly to introduce his Skytrain service which drastically changed aviation thinking. He also breeds and races horses. He was knighted in 1978.

21   Sir Freddie Laker.   Company chairman.   Gatwick, London

22 Sir William Walton, OM. Composer. Royal Albert Hall, London

'His music has always been a joy to me, and the man himself was not a disappointment. We wanted a photograph that counted, and we were able to do it in the Royal Albert Hall. I asked if the orchestra stands could be set out with music by Walton, and the picture began to take shape immediately. Walton, in spite of poor health, was tremendously co-operative. It was very touching to see the great affection the staff at the Royal Albert Hall had for him.'

William Walton was born in 1902 and educated at the Cathedral Choir School and Christ Church, Oxford. Among his many celebrated orchestral compositions are 'Facade', 'Belshazzar's Feast', 'Crown Imperial', 'Troilus and Cressida', his concerti for viola, violin and violoncello. Among his film scores are 'Henry V', 'Hamlet' and 'Richard III' for Laurence Olivier. He now lives in Italy. He was knighted in 1951 and received the Order of Merit in 1967.

'I appeared with eight other photographers in a series of lectures sponsored by the Royal Photographic Society, and it was there that I met my fellow speakers, Duffy, Bailey and Donovan, affectionately known in the profession as "The Terrible Trio", who had shaken up and influenced not only English photography, but also that of the whole world as well. We viewed each other with suspicion at first, and then we found out that the other guy was not only human, but worth drinking with, and for one solid week we enjoyed each other's company exchanging ideas about life and photography. To celebrate our marvellous week of conviviality and comradeship I decided to photograph them, in Duffy's studio. The photographic black border and frame number have far more meaning because it is a portrait of photographers. In the upper right hand corner there is the back of a flat marked "Top 3". This was strictly an accident. I didn't notice it until afterwards.'

Duffy (his little-used first name is Brian), David Bailey and Terence Donovan share similar backgrounds – all were London youths who worked at some time for John French. In the Sixties their fashion photography made a considerable impact, forcing attitudes to change. All have expanded beyond photography into the cinema and television and other media. Donovan is said to have made 900 television commercials.

23   David Bailey, Duffy, Terence Donovan.   Photographers.   Swiss Cottage, London

'Like so many others I succumb to Lord Goodman's charm, wit and intellect. I wanted to get the comfortable feeling of his London flat, and as the rooms are not all that large I threw open the double doors between his drawing room and study, getting them together in perspective. Lord Goodman is rather a large man, but the chair so totally engulfed him that he became almost lost in the comfortable leather. I tried to show something of his great wit and humour in this portrait.'

Lord Goodman's interests are broader than those of most distinguished men. He is a lawyer, and senior partner of Goodman, Derrick & Co. Since 1976 he has been Master of University College, Oxford. He has been Chairman of the Arts Council, the Observer Trust, the Newspaper Publishers' Association, British Lion Films, and the Theatres' Trust, among others. He has been Director of the Royal Opera House, the English National Opera and a Governor of the Royal Shakespeare Theatre. He is also President of the National Book League. He was born Arnold Goodman in 1913, and educated at the University of London and Downing College, Cambridge. He was made a Life Peer in 1965.

24 Lord Goodman, CH.   Lawyer.   Portland Place, London

'This is a photograph that I had been planning to do for several years, ever since I saw them working together in Pinter's *No Man's Land*. Their acting relationship, going back a lifetime, created a marvellous interplay that would have been a delight for any photographer to interpret. The picture was taken in an alleyway at the side of the Duke of York's Theatre where Gielgud was appearing. I feel that it could almost be directed by Pinter. We were set up and ready when they came along rather happily after a convivial lunch at the Garrick Club. They sailed right into the spirit of the occasion, and not only acted for me, but rather over-acted. The most startling bit of business was Sir Ralph's imitation of John Wayne.'

Sir John Gielgud was knighted in 1953 and made a Companion of Honour in 1977. He was born in 1904 and educated at Westminster. His first stage appearance was at the Old Vic in 1921. His long theatrical and film career has embraced many classical and modern roles and he has also directed many plays in London and New York.

Sir Ralph Richardson was knighted in 1947. He was born in 1902, and educated at Xaverian College, Brighton, where he made his first stage appearance in 1921. He made his first film in 1933. Sir John and Sir Ralph two of Britain's most distinguished actors.

25 Sir John Gielgud, Sir Ralph Richardson.   Actors.   Duke of York's Theatre, London

'If we had shot this in a chapel it might have had a more religious aspect, but I felt that as we had three different faiths the background should be neutral. It is in fact a corridor in Lambeth Palace. The mood is influenced by the light coming in through the window. The shadows are dark but there is a warmth and friendliness. Aware of the different branches of the church represented here I told them I wanted to make the picture non-denominational. With crisp logic, Cardinal Hume, resplendent in his scarlet robes, looked at me with a twinkle and said: "And how do you propose to do that?" I couldn't think of a quick answer. Later, as I was making a Polaroid to check the lighting, I said: "This is the only time when a photographer prays, when he is taking a photograph." There was a pause, then the Archbishop of Canterbury turned to the others and said: "Gentlemen, I think we should do something about Mr Newman!"'

Dr Donald Coggan has been Archbishop of Canterbury since 1974. From 1961 until 1974 he was Archbishop of York. He was born in 1909 and educated at Merchant Taylors' and St John's College, Cambridge, and Wycliffe Hall, Oxford.

Basil, Cardinal Hume became Archbishop of Westminster in 1976. He was born in 1923, educated at Ampleforth, St Benet's Hall, Oxford, and Fribourg University. He became a priest in 1950 and returned to Ampleforth as a teacher in 1952. He was a housemaster 1955–63 and Abbott 1963–76.

The Rev Stanley Turl was the Moderator of the Free Church Council from March 1978 until March 1979.

These three men are the heads of the main national Christian communities.

26 Most Rev and Rt Hon Dr Donald Coggan, Archbishop of Canterbury. Rev Stanley Turl,
Moderator of Free Church Council. His Eminence Basil Cardinal Hume, Archbishop of Westminster.
Lambeth Palace, London

'He understood exactly what I had in mind, and went along with the concept. I suppose that you could go on indefinitely with visual puns about big wheels and power symbols. For me, I was simply using the door to the strong room as a design device to give strength to the picture, as well as an environmental symbol.'

William Armstrong was born in 1915 and educated at Bec School, London, and Exeter College, Oxford. He entered the Civil Service in 1938, and 1968–74 was the Official Head of the Home Civil Service. He was knighted in 1963 and created a Life Peer in 1975. Since 1975 he has been Chairman of the Midland Bank.

27   Lord Armstrong.   Head of the Civil Service 1968–74.   City of London.

'There were so many ways to photograph Betjeman. Many people think of him in the context of Victorian architecture. A poet, however, lives within his own mind, and we decided to do the picture in his home, a little house in Chelsea which is like a dolls' house filled with books. As the photograph shows, he is a man filled with laughter. The thing that delighted me was his enthusiasm and humour. You would think that someone of his age and attainment would be full of cynicism, but no, his delight at the world was without limitations. He was extremely modest and even humble, and greeted me with great excitement that I was to do his photograph.'

John Betjeman was born in 1906 and educated at Marlborough and Oxford. Since 1972 he has been Poet Laureate. He is an authority on country churches and Victorian railway stations, and his writings demonstrate his sensitive visual taste and his keen perception of middle-class attitudes. His verse autobiography, 'Summoned by Bells', was published in 1960. He received his knighthood in 1969.

28   Sir John Betjeman.   Poet Laureate.   Chelsea, London

'It was easy to understand the admiration the British had for her. I was in a quandary after looking around her home to see how I would take the photograph. Upstairs was devoted to memorabilia of her fabulous career, but was the repository of the past rather than something she and her husband had chosen to live with today. For this reason I felt I could photograph her in her wonderful, cluttered drawing room with stuffed furniture, books and pictures, in the attitude of someone living in the present. We reached rapport and I photographed her as a rather happy person. As I began to take my last exposures I became uncomfortable and I realised I was getting quite ill. For the next hour Dame Vera and her husband were mopping my brow. After returning to London and seeing a doctor I crawled into bed. It was just an upset stomach, but I had the strange, but pleasant, experience of being ministered to by one of Britain's heroines, and by now certainly mine as well.'

Vera Lynn was born in 1917, made her singing debut at the age of 7, and her first broadcast in 1935. From 1937 to 1940 she sang with the Ambrose Orchestra, then went solo, and became known from her radio programme 'Sincerely Yours', which ran through the war years, as the 'Forces' Sweetheart'. She is an enduring show business personality and the first British performer to have an American Number One record. The best known of her many songs is probably 'We'll Meet Again'.

29　Dame Vera Lynn.　Singer.　Ditchling, Sussex

30   Chris Bonington.   Mountaineer.   Wigton, Cumbria

'The only day we could get to him was the very day he was leaving for London en route for the Himalayas and the tragic K2 attempt. We took a train to Carlisle and drove out to the village where he lives, and found a location fifteen minutes from his home – a group of rocks where he practises mountain-climbing. It would have been very simple to have photographed him in close-up with maps and ropes and so on, but this was not my intention. I wanted to recreate the atmosphere of a climb, rather than a specific locale.'

Chris Bonington was born in 1934 and educated at University College School, London, and the Royal Military Academy, Sandhurst. Since 1962 he has been a mountaineer, writer and photographer. Among his famous climbs are Annapurna II, Mont Blanc, and North Wall Eiger (first British ascent), and he led the British Everest Expeditions of 1972 and 1975.

'I have photographed seven presidents, but there is something special about 10 Downing Street. Even the Prime Minister was moved as he outlined to me the history that had been made in the Cabinet Room. At first we could not get permission to photograph there, but I made it clear that I wanted a picture in a working setting, not in one of the elegant, but anonymous state rooms at Number Ten. Once we convinced them, we set to work, observing the protocol, problems of security, and making sure that the detectives guarding the Prime Minister's body did not get in the line of shooting. Mr Callaghan took a great interest in the session and a few days later I took the photographs round to Number Ten to show him, at his request. After half-an-hour with him an anxious secretary appeared with batches of urgent papers for signature, concerned that the Prime Minister had been tied up so long with a photographer!'

James Callaghan, born 1912, entered Parliament in 1945 after wartime service in the Royal Navy. From 1964 to 1967 he was Chancellor of the Exchequer, Home Secretary 1967–70, Foreign Secretary 1974–6. He became Prime Minister in 1976 after the resignation of Sir Harold Wilson, and at the same time became leader of the Labour Party.

31 Rt Hon James Callaghan. Prime Minister 1976–9. Downing Street, London

'I have photographed Henry Moore on a number of occasions, going back to 1946. I cannot think of anyone more modest and self-effacing. This time I selected a great structure he had put up in the grounds of his house for the purpose of doing a sculpture for Lincoln Center in New York, which until recently I could look down on from my bedroom. It made a marvellous abstraction in the background, together with the large chunks of styrofoam he uses to block out the beginnings of a large sculpture. There was a note from the past in the shape of his famous reclining figure in the background. The picture was taken shortly after his 80th birthday celebration and exhibit in Kensington Gardens and the Serpentine Gallery, which used a photograph of mine for the posters.'

Henry Moore was born in Yorkshire in 1898, and was educated at Castleford Grammar School. After army service 1917–19 he studied at Leeds School of Art and the Royal College of Art. During the Second World War he was an official war artist. He is Britain's greatest living sculptor and his monolithic works can be found in many countries of the world. His first London exhibition was in 1928. Fifty years later the world celebrated his 80th birthday as many of his works were displayed in Kensington Gardens and the Tate Gallery. He was made a Companion of Honour in 1956 and awarded the Order of Merit in 1963.

32   Henry Moore, OM, CH.   Sculptor.   Much Hadham, Herts

'I believe that these men look very much what they are. There was a problem in finding a location, but the library at Christ Church was a photographer's dream. However, our first difficulty came when we had problems with the electric current and our bulbs kept exploding, which meant that eventually we had too few to fill in the background. The next big problem was organising the men to be there on time and to give us the allotted twenty-five minutes. Unhappily, one showed up late and to everybody's astonishment announced that he had to leave in ten minutes. After we continued to photograph he simply got up and walked out. Anticipating this I had already got the picture I wanted. But you always find one person who finds it difficult to go along with everyone else. I must say that I enjoyed the company of all the others very much.'

The Rev Canon Peter Baelz is a Canon of Christ Church, and Regius Professor of Moral and Pastoral Theology.

The Rev Professor James Barr is a Student of Christ Church, and the Regius Professor of Hebrew.

Professor Sir Richard Doll is a Student of Christ Church, and the Regius Professor of Medicine.

Professor Antony Honoré is a Fellow of All Souls, and Regius Professor of Civil Law.

Professor Hugh Lloyd-Jones is a Student of Christ Church, and Regius Professor of Greek.

The Rev Professor John McManners is a Canon of Christ Church and Regius Professor of Ecclesiastical History.

Professor Hugh Trevor-Roper is a Fellow of Oriel College, and the Regius Professor of Modern History.

The Rev Professor Maurice Wiles is a Canon of Christ Church, and Regius Professor of Divinity.

The Regius Professors of Oxford are appointed by the Crown.

33   Prof Hugh Lloyd-Jones, Prof Sir Richard Doll, Rev Canon Peter Baelz, Rev Prof Maurice
Wiles, Rev Prof John McManners, Rev Prof James Barr, Prof Hugh Trevor-Roper, Prof Antony
Honoré.   Regius Professors.   Christ Church, Oxford

'I didn't know what to expect. What does a middle-aged photographer whose taste runs more to classical music expect from one of the Beatles? However, we were greeted warmly at his unbelievable mansion at Henley, a perfectly restored Victorian building with gargoyles and carved mahogany staircases. Upstairs was one of the most complicated arrays of recording equipment I have ever seen and a studio where George Harrison cuts his records. I had a great deal of fun photographing him against the lights of the console. We were impressed with his seriousness and his perception of the pressures of the music business. But if he didn't know about them, who would?'

George Harrison was born in Liverpool in 1943. During the Sixties he was lead guitar for the Beatles, a group of legendary accomplishment in the history of popular music. Since its break-up he has concentrated on a solo career of composition and recording.

George Harrison.   Musician and Composer. Henley-on-Thames, Oxon

Lord Home. Prime Minister 1963–4. Westminster, London

'I can now understand the word "gentleman", having met Lord Home. He is a man concerned about the feelings of others and desirous to help. I was unable to arrange a suitable background at the House of Lords, and after shooting I confess that I didn't think I had made a satisfactory photograph. Lord Home immediately said "Let's do it again". I saw the Royal Gallery and then made arrangements for us to photograph there at a later date, early in the morning. Technically it was interesting. I prefer to use available or existing light. It would have been utterly impossible to have lit this big room to retain the atmosphere. There was not enough light at the end I was photographing him to balance so I used two small spotlights and exposures of up to four seconds to overcome the low light level. It was astonishing that Lord Home could hold a pose for so long.'

Lord Home succeeded to the title of 14th Earl of Home on the death of his father, but in 1963 renounced his title for life when he became Prime Minister, and was then Sir Alec Douglas-Home. He was made a Life Peer in 1974. He was born in 1903, educated at Eton and Christ Church, and first entered Parliament in 1931. From 1960 to 1963 he was Foreign Secretary, and led the Conservative Party 1963–5. From 1970 to 1974 he was again Foreign Secretary.

'We all had fun with this. I watched a number of their tapes in order to get the feeling and quality of their work, which I enjoyed thoroughly, when I saw them in tails I thought that this is the way I had to photograph them. We gleefully worked together as though we had a relationship of many years' standing. I deliberately used a photographic device, a simple no-seam white background. The picture was shot in the Floral Hall adjoining the Royal Opera House, and they used the large gentlemen's cloakroom in the lobby to change into their white ties and tails. Unfortunately, it was the time of day when the cleaning ladies have control of the Opera House, and one barged in with her bucket and mop, took one look and fled yelling "Blimey! Morecambe and Wise is in the Gent's!"'

Eric Morecambe was born in the seaside resort of that name in 1926 (his real name is Bartholomew). He first teamed with Ernie Wise in 1941 at the Liverpool Empire and they made their first broadcast in 1943. It was television that brought them to the height of their fame and established them as leading British comedians. Ernie Wise (real name Wiseman) was born in 1924.

36 Eric Morecambe, Ernie Wise. Comedians. Covent Garden, London

'I knew his music, but just to clarify my attitudes I refreshed my memory by listening to some of his recordings a day or so earlier. We lunched at his house in Wiltshire, looking across a beautiful English landscape. His studio was the room below with the same view, the piano in front of a big picture window. The relationship of these strong, hard, abstract lines and the bucolic landscape make the picture. I deliberately did not crop the window frame, otherwise it would have looked as if I had dragged him with the piano into the garden, like an advertising shot.'

Michael Tippett was born in 1905. He was educated at Stamford Grammar School and the Royal College of Music. His first major work was the oratorio 'A Child of our Time' first performed in 1944, followed by his Symphony No 1 in the following year. His other works include the operas 'The Midsummer Marriage', 'King Priam' and 'The Ice Break', three piano sonatas and three more symphonies. He was knighted in 1966.

37 **Sir Michael Tippett. Composer. Chippenham, Wilts**

'It was a deliberate decision to gather these three Nobel prizewinners together in a typical Cambridge setting that would not only be magnificent but also represent the men. We therefore chose the Wren Library at Trinity, a superb stage set on which to work. The men lent a great human quality and contrast to this very beautiful interior. It was a great opportunity to make use of perspective. Of course, one has to go back to Frans Hals and Rembrandt who laid the groundwork for putting a group together.'

Sir Alan Hodgkin is the Master of Trinity College, Cambridge. In 1963 he was joint winner of the Nobel Prize for Medicine. He was born in 1914.

Lord Todd was Master of Christ's College, Cambridge 1963–78 and was Professor of Organic Chemistry at the University 1944–71. In 1957 he won the Nobel Prize for Chemistry. Since 1975 he has been President of the Royal Society. He was born in 1907. He was made a Life Peer in 1962 and received the Order of Merit in 1977.

Sir Nevill Mott was Cavendish Professor of Physics 1954–71. In 1977 he won the Nobel Prize for Physics. He was born in 1905.

38   Sir Alan Hodgkin, OM, Lord Todd, OM, Sir Nevill Mott.   Nobel prizewinning scientists.
Trinity College, Cambridge

39   Sir Peter Pears.   Singer.   Snape, Suffolk

'Involved arrangements were made for me to photograph him at the Maltings at Snape to represent him and his lifelong creative relationship with Benjamin Britten, which culminated in this beautiful hall. On arrival and walking around I became excited by the marshes and began to plan to do a couple of pictures outside. I then found that I had no choice. The Maltings were in the hands of a rock group and BBC Television. These marshes reminded me strongly of *Peter Grimes*, and I was also reminded of the photographs of Emerson, in Norfolk. My picture was taken at sundown which gave me a beautiful light, but we had to move rapidly.'

Peter Pears was born in 1910 and educated at Lancing, Oxford and the Royal College of Music. He joined the BBC Singers in 1934, and in 1939 began American and European tours with Benjamin Britten, with whom he founded the Aldeburgh Festival in 1948. He first sang many new works by Britten, Tippett, Berkeley and other British composers. His best-known operatic performance was the title role in Britten's 'Peter Grimes'. He was knighted in 1978.

'This picture was taken on the stage of the Garrick Theatre, where Pinter's *The Homecoming* was being revived. We turned away from the set though, because I wanted the symbolic atmosphere of the theatre, rather than a specific play. I was influenced by my great love for the English theatre and my admiration for the work of these two men, whom I wanted to represent equally. They had become players on a stage. Pinter was somewhat reticent, while Stoppard was extremely relaxed and in a jocular mood. I tried them both ways round – one sitting, the other standing, but I found this picture the most successful of the two positions.'

Harold Pinter was born in 1930 and educated at Hackney Downs Grammar School. From 1949 until 1957 he was an actor, mostly in repertory. His plays include 'The Birthday Party', 'The Caretaker', 'The Homecoming', 'Old Times', 'No Man's Land'. He has written several screenplays and has directed for stage and film. Since 1973 he has been Associate Director of the National Theatre.

Tom Stoppard was born in 1937 and was initially a journalist of the 'Western Daily Press' and the 'Bristol Evening World'. His best-known plays are 'Rosencrantz and Guildenstern are Dead', 'The Real Inspector Hound', 'Travesties', 'Jumpers', 'Dirty Linen' and 'Night and Day'.

40   Tom Stoppard, Harold Pinter.   Playwrights.   Garrick Theatre, London

'Physically he is a Dickens character and plays the part. He is delightful, with a searching manner to see what kind of a response he can elicit. I found him marvellous to work with because he understood what I wanted and reacted with even greater flair than an actor. He loved cigars, which made him an immediate favourite of mine, and I insisted upon his smoking all the way through the sitting so that he felt comfortable. The biggest problem I had was in selecting the final image, for there were so many good ones. He did not give me the impression of being frail – more of a battleship that was slowing up a little bit – but not too much.'

John Boynton Priestley was born in Bradford in 1894. He was educated there and at Trinity Hall, Cambridge. He served in the Army in the First World War and his first work was published in 1922. He established himself as an all-round literary figure – novelist, playwright, essayist and broadcaster. Amidst his prolific output his best-known work is probably 'The Good Companions', a novel which was later dramatised and filmed. He received the Order of Merit in 1977.

41 J. B. Priestley, OM. Author. Alverston, Stratford-upon-Avon, Warwicks

'The piano has always been to me one of the most beautiful objects ever made for utilitarian purposes. The Bechstein in Dame Janet's home is used here symbolically, although of course she works with it when she is practising. She was quite stiff in the beginning and admitted to not liking her picture being taken, but I think that this comes from some rather poor ones that I had seen in the past. As we got started she began to relax, and eventually we were in a rather happy, jovial mood and were having a great deal of fun, which I think the picture reflects. I think that this is an important part of the photographer's function, not only understanding putting the picture together graphically, but also having an ability to work and relax his subjects so that they become what they are, and lose self-consciousness.'

Janet Baker was born in 1933 and educated at the College for Girls, York, and Wintringham, Grimsby. A singer of rare tonal quality and resonance, she has won many international prizes, starting with the Kathleen Ferrier award in 1956. That enabled her to study in Salzburg. She was made a Dame of the British Empire in 1976.

42 Dame Janet Baker. Singer. Harrow, London

'We carried the heavy cases of equipment for this Polacolor shot up to David Hockney's fifth-floor studio, which is full of daylight. The bulk of the lighting in this shot is with strobe, giving a strong imitation of the natural north light. Virtually everything in the shot was there in the studio with the exception of the painting there on the right. I felt that this Mondrianesque composition required a breaking up of the space. I don't suppose anyone will believe me when I say that the only Hockney painting that seemed to work showed a Polaroid camera on a tripod!'

David Hockney was born in Bradford in 1937, and educated at Bradford Grammar School, Bradford School of Art and the Royal College of Art. He is the leader of the younger generation of British painters, renowned for his high quality of figurative drawing, striking use of colour and adventurous sense of composition. In 1975 a film 'A Bigger Splash' was based on his work, with particular reference to a specific painting.

David Hockney.   Artist. Bayswater, London

Lord Mountbatten. Admiral of the Fleet. Romsey, Hants

'We travelled down to Hampshire to photograph him at Broadlands. We found him revelling in the intricacies of a new copying machine. We had a very entertaining lunch where we realised how acutely perceptive was his interest in world affairs. I decided on two photographic approaches, one using the decorative features of one of the rooms in the very beautiful old house, and the other outside where, in his full-dress uniform of Admiral of the Fleet he was framed by the columns of the portico, with the rolling landscape of his estate beyond. Thus we showed Mountbatten the admiral and the country squire.'

Lord Mountbatten, whose earldom was created in 1947, was born at Windsor in 1900, and is the great-grandson of Queen Victoria. He was educated at Locker's Park, Osborne, the Royal Naval College, Dartmouth, and Christ's College, Cambridge. He saw active service in the First World War as a midshipman, accompanied the Prince of Wales on his tours around the world in the Twenties, commanded HMS Kelly in 1939 and was torpedoed, later commanded Combined Operations and in 1943 became Supreme Commander, SE Asia. After the war he was the last Viceroy of India, and after independence Mountbatten became the first Governor-General.

'This picture proves one thing – a stereotype of any profession just doesn't work. Can you imagine five more different men? We had to photograph the publishers on neutral ground, so we chose the library of the National Book League. There was friendly (one wonders how friendly?) joking as I positioned them carefully into different places. Rather than assign the ladder I asked if there were any volunteers. Lord Longford then chose the position.'

André Deutsch founded the company which bears his name, and of which he is chairman and managing director, in 1951. He was born in 1917 and educated in Budapest, Vienna and Zurich.

Paul Hamlyn was born in 1926 and educated at St Christopher's, Letchworth. He founded the Hamlyn Publishing Group which was acquired by IPC in 1964. Since 1971 he has been chairman of Octopus Books which he founded.

Lord Longford, born 1905, educated Eton and New College, Oxford, is, among his many accomplishments, a publisher. His company is Sidgwick & Jackson.

Charles Pick was born in 1917 and was educated at the Masonic School, Bushey. He is managing director of the Heinemann Group.

Lord Weidenfeld was born in 1919 and educated in Vienna. He founded Weidenfeld & Nicolson in 1948 and has been chairman ever since.

45   André Deutsch, Paul Hamlyn, Charles Pick, Lord Longford, Lord Weidenfeld.
Publishers.   National Book League, London

'Where else could one plan to photograph him except in the Olivier Theatre? We arranged the picture in between the matinée and evening performance of *King Lear*, which left only an hour between the cleaning ladies and Olivier's visit to hospital. There was much excitement and emotion at his appearance in the theatre. Because of the technical difficulty in lighting the huge space and keeping the atmosphere, long exposures had to be used. When we had finished, Olivier, obviously exhausted, shook hands with all those who had waited to say goodbye to him. We watched him walk across the stage, hesitate and take one last look at the auditorium before vanishing into the wings.'

Laurence Olivier was born in 1907 and first appeared on the stage in 1922, playing Katherine in a boys' version of 'The Taming of the Shrew'. Among his first successes was Stanhope in 'Journey's End'. He moved rapidly from matinée idol to Britain's leading Shakespearean actor, and has produced, directed and acted in many major productions. He has also maintained a steady film career, overcoming early typecasting as a romantic hero, particularly by Hollywood. His 'Henry V', 'Hamlet' and 'Richard III' are milestones of British cinema. He was the first director of the National Theatre, and the largest of the three auditoria in the South Bank complex is named after him. He was knighted in 1947, and became a Life Peer in 1970.

46   Lord Olivier.   Actor and director.   National Theatre, London

'She still is an enigma to me, even after meeting her. When we met she was warm and friendly, but when I set the camera up she withdrew behind a shield. She preferred not to be photographed at home, rather at her publisher's offices, which immediately set her apart, requiring that I photograph her more as an abstraction than a realistic study. The offices were being painted at the time, and the unreality of the long hallway with the painters' drip cloth on the floor made the environment surreal. It would be very easy to photograph Ms Murdoch as a bland hausfrau, but her distanced attitude in this picture is a representation of her and her work, a barrier between her and you.'

Iris Murdoch was born in Dublin in 1919. She was educated at Badminton and Somerville, Oxford. Since 1948 she has been a Fellow of St Anne's College, Oxford. She is a philosopher and a leading British novelist. Her best-known works include 'The Sandcastle', 'A Severed Head', 'The Italian Girl' and 'An Accidental Man'. In 1978 she won the Booker Prize for 'The Sea, the Sea'.

47   Iris Murdoch.   Author and philosopher.   Chatto and Windus, London

'Shooting this was a nightmare. Getting them all together was probably the technical feat of the century. We finally settled on the Spanish Grand Prix in which both Hunt and Surtees were participating, and Stewart was the guest of the King. Stirling Moss very sportingly travelled to Madrid for us. A Grand Prix is like a circus, and I quickly realised that to get all four of these men together in a public place would be to incite a riot. I soon located a white tent attached to James Hunt's trailer which would give both a soft light and, I thought, some privacy. Unfortunately, the news of the four of them together got around, and it was all we could do to keep people from crawling under the tent flaps and interfering with the shooting. It was a miracle that any photograph could be made with the mob screaming to be allowed in.'

James Hunt was World Motor Racing Champion in 1976 and has won 11 Grands Prix.

Stirling Moss, although never World Champion, won 16 Grands Prix and 178 other races before retiring in 1962.

Jackie Stewart was World Champion in 1969, 1971 and 1973 and has won 27 Grands Prix, an unbeaten record.

John Surtees was a world champion motor cyclist six times before turning to motor racing. He was World Champion in 1964, and has won 6 Grands Prix.

48 Jackie Stewart, Stirling Moss, John Surtees, James Hunt.
Grand Prix drivers.   Madrid, Spain

'We met at the Medical Research Center at the University of Miami – the same university where I began my art studies in the mid Thirties. He was there to deliver a talk for an international scientific conference. We met for dinner after his late arrival and selected his "work clothes" for the shot the next morning. Neither of us were happy about the crack of dawn appointment, but the conference officials re-scheduled the next day's events to suit us. The problem was to create the general look of the laboratories he had occupied over the years. I abstracted the ever-present scientist's tool – the blackboard – and held it to a more symbolic concept by having Dr Crick work out some problems and then erase them almost to obscurity. But the principal emphasis is on his own ebullient, slyly humorous personality.'

Francis Crick was born in 1916 and educated at Mill Hill, University College, London and Gonville & Caius College, Cambridge. He is one of the greatest living authorities on molecular and cell biology and in 1962 shared the Nobel Prize for Medicine for his work in determining the molecular structure of DNA, the chemical that constitutes the gene, and showing how genetic characteristics are passed from generation to generation. Since 1977 he has been the J. W. Kieckhefer Distinguished Professor at the Salk Institute, San Diego, California.

49   **Francis Crick.   Scientist.   University of Miami, Coral Gables, Florida**

'I'd never really met Beaton, although I have admired his work for as long as I have been a photographer. My working approach is so much different from his. When we went to his home he was recovering from a severe illness. I took the liberty of photographing him with a slight exaggeration of his elegance and style, and he went along with it. Since that happy day we have developed quite a pen-pal relationship.'

Cecil Beaton was born in 1904 and educated at Harrow and Cambridge. A brilliant photographer and stage designer with a great sense of style, he is also the author of many books, beginning with 'The Book of Beauty' in 1930. Most people are aware of his striking costumes and sets for both the stage and cinema versions of 'My Fair Lady'. He was knighted in 1972.

50   **Sir Cecil Beaton.**   **Photographer and designer.**   **Broadchalke, Salisbury, Wilts**

Index

This book was designed by Michael Rand and edited by George Perry, both of *The Sunday Times*. The exhibition *The Great British* was organised by Colin Ford, Keeper of Film and Photography at the National Portrait Gallery. Staff at *The Sunday Times* who worked on the project include Christine Walker, researcher; June Stanier, picture editor; Gilvrie Misstear, art editor; Mary Hodges, Jane Charteris and Sarah-Jane Prior, research and administration. Special thanks are due to Chris Nation and George Hewitt, assistants to Arnold Newman; Adrian Ensor, processing, and Frank J. Iannotti and Tom Okada of Newman Studios, New York. The project would not have been possible without the encouragement of Harold Evans, Editor of *The Sunday Times*, Ron Hall, Editor of *The Sunday Times Magazine*, and Dr John Hayes, Director of The National Portrait Gallery.

The photographs of Bill Brandt and David Hockney are Polacolor prints